Five Areas Of Focus For Superachieving

CHRISTINA M. EANES

Table of Contents

Introduction   1

Section One: Mindset   3

Lesson One: Got Metacognition?   5

Lesson Two: Don't Listen to the Negative Voices!   12

Lesson Three: Get a Reality Check   19

Lesson Four: Choose Your Stories Carefully   25

Section Two: Resilience   30

Lesson One: Adversity is a Gift   32

Lesson Two: Emotions Are Data   37

Lesson Three: Seek Internal Fulfillment   42

Section Three: Connection   47

Lesson One: Connecting With Others Is Non-Negotiable   49

Lesson Two: Get A Fan Club   53

Lesson Three: Find A Champion   58

Lesson Four: Be Selective of the Company You Keep   61

Section Four: Self-Care   67

Lesson One: Nurture Mind, Body, and Soul   69

Lesson Two: My Body Is My Temple   73

Lesson Three: Don't Have Enough Time? Bulls%#@!   77

Section Five: Self-Development   81

Lesson One: For Goodness' Sake, Get Some Coaching!   83

Lesson Two: Enlighten Me!   88

Lesson Three: Study Your Greats   91

Bringing It All Together   95

Introduction

There is only one corner of the universe you can be certain of improving, and that's your own self.

—Aldous Huxley

Welcome to *Quit Bleeping Around: Five Areas of Focus for Superachieving*. Consider this your guidebook in getting out of your own way and stepping up your game to achieve more of what you want in life – personally and professionally.

This guidebook is based on the book *Quit Bleeping Around: 77 Secrets to Superachieving*. Most of the 77 secrets can be mapped out into five specific areas of focus that will help you launch your achievement efforts. These five areas each have their own section in this book. They are:

1. *Mindset*: This is foundational for achieving more in life! In this focus area, you will learn how your mind can either help or hinder you in achieving what you want in life. You will also learn strategies for getting out of your own way and harnessing the amazing power of your mind.

2. *Resilience*: How you see adversity in your life determines your level of success. In this focus area, you will learn how to increase your resilience.

3. *Connection*: Connecting with others is not only essential to achieving your goals and dreams, but also to being a human being. In this focus area, you will have the opportunity to examine how you connect with others, and to develop a strategy for both increasing your connections, as well as being more effective in connecting with others.

4. *Self-care*: Effectively tending to your mind, body, and soul is crucial to achieving more in your life. In this focus area, you examine your current levels of health in these areas and develop strategies for improving them.

5. *Self-development*: Continually developing oneself is vital to stepping up one's achievement efforts. The work you will do in this focus area helps you set up a game plan for your personal and professional development.

Instructions for Moving Forward

This guidebook is meant to take some time to go through – how much depends on you and the level of work you would like to invest in each area. Please go through each section carefully and take the time to do the work in each *Deepen the Learning* section. This is an investment in yourself to achieve your goals, and yes - your dreams, more effectively. It is guaranteed that what you learn in this guidebook about yourself will help you in life in general – your relationships, the way you communicate, your confidence levels, how you show up in life, and the impact you have on others.

You are a superachiever after all – someone who wants to make a positive impact on our world while growing themselves in the process.

Section One: Mindset

Welcome to the first section of this guidebook, which is all about the mindset. Although all five areas of focus are important, this one is absolutely key to achieving more in life.

In the first lesson, we cover *Secret #17: Got Metacognition?* Here, you will examine how your thinking is leading to your current results and develop strategies for getting the results you desire.

In the second lesson, we cover *Secret #16: Don't Listen to the Negative Voices!* In this lesson, you identify and actually name the negative voices in your head and develop strategies for reducing the impact they have on you.

In the third lesson, we cover *Secret #26: Get a Reality Check!* In this lesson, we cover the steps involved when you create a belief, specifically one that is limiting you, and how you can use those same steps to change your perspective.

In the final lesson, we cover *Secret #40: Choose Your Stories Carefully*. You have the power to create your own reality, and you need to use your powers for good. In this lesson, you are given a strategy for changing those stories that aren't serving you.

Lesson One: Got Metacognition?

Welcome to the first lesson, where we focus on *Secret #17: Got Metacognition?*

For our first lesson in this section, we cover "metacognition" - which is essentially thinking about your thinking. This is a very important skill for superachievers to have because self-awareness is the path to getting out of your own way.

What you see below is a model that summarizes the work of former Harvard professor Chris Arygris. The model demonstrates that an observer (that's you), takes action (based on our thinking), and then gets results.

If observer in the model takes action which results in failure, there are generally three common ways an individual will respond.

1. The first response to failure is to consider it an external issue that one has no control over. Such as, "I didn't get promoted because they don't like me - there's nothing I can do about it." Not a very powerful place to be!

2. The next typical response is to keep trying different actions to get different results. This is often a waste of time and energy because it is a non-strategic trial-and-error tactic.

3. The final response, and one that is not utilized as often as it should be, is to go back and examine how one's thoughts led to the results experienced. This is a much more powerful position, because having the ability to examine and change one's thoughts can literally change reality.

Let's explore an example of how the third response looks in action. Jenny believed that she wanted a promotion in her office. So, she applied for any promotional position that came open whether it was something she wanted to do or not. Jenny failed in obtaining several positions before she decided to try something new – metacognition. Jenny took time to reflect on how her thinking led to her current results and decided to look at things differently, using the multiple perspectives technique you will soon learn. Jenny decided that she was greatly limiting herself by only applying to positions in her office. Even though she liked the office and the people she worked with, she was ready for a more challenging position. She broadened her perspective and started looking at other divisions within her current organization that were still within her field of expertise as well as other companies within a 20-mile radius of her home. Not long after, Jenny found a nice promotional opportunity just five minutes from her home!

Deepen the Learning

It's time to apply this concept to your thinking. In the following exercises you will go through several steps. The first step is to identify a current goal and consider your perspective on it. Then identify three to five different ways of looking at your goal. Let's look at example of what Jenny did to change her perspective.

Jenny chose four different perspectives to help her get out of her thinking rut. She chose a cloud, her cat, her mentor from college, and Ellen DeGeneres. The sillier the better because sometimes your brain needs a reboot to get out of the deep neural pathway it has created.

- When Jenny looked at her challenge from the cloud's perspective, she saw that she didn't need to limit herself so much. She saw clouds as being able to move from one place to another based on the air currents.

- When Jenny looked at her challenge from her cat's perspective, she realized she needed to chill out a bit, take a break, and be more strategic about getting a promotion. She loves how her cat will play when she wants, nap when she wants, and go about her day in how she sees fit.

- When Jenny looked at her challenge from her former college mentor's perspective, she realized that the previous good advice he had given her on paying her dues to get promoted in the office she worked in had stuck with her and was holding her back with this challenge.

- When Jenny looked at her challenge from the perspective of one of her favorite comedians/talk show hosts, Ellen DeGeneres, she decided that it was time to broaden her perspective and look at different companies for a promotion within her field. She laughed as she envisioned Ellen telling her, "What's the problem? Go somewhere else!"

Jenny received new information from each of the perspectives she tried. Sometimes when going through this process, individuals find that only one perspective resonates with them.

Regardless of how many different viewpoints you can obtain from this exercise, it will help broaden your perspective.

Now it's your turn - explore various perspectives of your choosing in relation to the challenge you are facing. Once you choose a new way of thinking, identify five steps in the next 90 days that you can take and add them to an action plan with due dates.

Secret #17: Got Metacognition?

What is your biggest goal in life right now? What do you want?

_____

_____

_____

_____

_____

_____

Identify (5) people, characters, or "things" and write down what their perceptions of your goal. We'll refer to these as "Alter Egos."

Alter Ego #1_____

_____

_____

_____

_____

_____

Alter Ego #2_____

_____

_____

_____

_____

Alter Ego #3_____

_____

_____

_____

_____

Alter Ego #4_____

_____

_____

_____

_____

Alter Ego #5_____

_____

_____

_____

_____

_____

Which of these identified perspectives resonates the most with you? Which one will help you move toward your goal more quickly?

_____

_____

_____

_____

_____

Identify (5) steps you will take in the next 90 days to make this happen:

_____

_____

_____

_____

_____

_____

_____

Draw a picture of the Alter Ego you chose:

Lesson One Reflections and Actions to Take

_____

_____

_____

_____

_____

_____

_____

_____

_____

_____

_____

_____

_____

_____

_____

_____

_____

Lesson Two: Don't Listen to the Negative Voices!

In the second lesson, we focus on *Secret #16: Don't Listen to the Negative Voices!*

Ughh! Those negative voices in our heads! Every one of us has them – no one truly escapes their grip. Some of us may be less in control of the voices, but we ALL have them.

You've probably heard of emotional intelligence, but have you heard of positive intelligence? Positive intelligence is looking at the percentage of time your mind serves you versus the percentage of time your mind sabotages you.

What are these voices saying? Well, we each have ones unique to us; however, there are some universal ones. These negative voices that you hear are aptly named – in the coaching world, we call them saboteurs or gremlins.

How did we develop these little buggers?

The mind is much like an iceberg – like the tip of the iceberg that is visible, only about 5 to 10% of our behaviors come from our conscious mind; while 90 to 95% of our behaviors come from our subconscious mind (depending on which research studies you consult). This is completely necessary – why? If you had to consciously think of each and every behavior you needed to get throughout the day, you'd be exhausted! Imagine putting all your focus and energy in the mechanics involved in brushing your teeth or tying your shoes.

To conserve energy, we've developed a program for successfully surviving situations we've faced in the past. Think of these as little computer programs we've written that are now stored in our subconscious. When we are faced with a situation that requires a response from us, our mind quickly searches through the databanks for when a similar situation occurred, pulls out the previous program we used to respond, and then runs it. Where we trip ourselves up is when we don't consider the effects these previously devised programs now have on us.

Here's the problem - We are keeping and running programs that are no longer serving us. Most of our saboteurs or gremlins were formed in early childhood to essentially help us survive it and make it to adulthood. For example, let's say little Susie developed a belief when she was five that she received more love and attention when she was a good girl and helped others. She also watched her mother work tirelessly to meet the needs of others before her own.

Then, little Susie grows up and brings the "Pleaser" saboteur with her to work. She doesn't know how to say no to others and will often take on a lot more than she can handle to feel appreciated.

Congratulations - we have officially survived childhood and the negative voices are no longer serving us. How do we minimize their impact on us? Quite simply, we shed some light on them.

Deepen the Learning

It's your turn! For the first part of your exercises below, you'll go to www.positiveintelligence.com and take the *Saboteur Assessment* to determine which of the ten saboteurs are lurking around in your subconscious. This is a complimentary assessment that provides you with a detailed report on each saboteur, why and how it shows up in our lives, as well as strategies for addressing it.

For the remainder of the assignment, you'll work with your top three saboteurs – examining how they have benefited you in the past; what triggers bring them out; and you can draw and name them. Visualizing your saboteurs takes some of their power away. Finally, you'll create an action plan for reining them in and implement it.

Secret #16: Don't Listen to the Negative Voices!

Go to www.positiveintelligence.com/assessments and take the Saboteur Assessment. List your top (3) saboteurs and how they are affecting your achievement efforts right now.

_____

_____

_____

_____

_____

_____

_____

How much of the "Judge" is showing up in your life right now? Are you judging yourself too much? What about your circumstances? Others?

_____

_____

_____

_____

_____

_____

_____

_____

Congratulations, you've survived childhood! You don't need the saboteurs to protect you anymore. In what ways do they keep trying to protect you, ending up harming you instead?

_____

_____

_____

_____

_____

_____

_____

For each of your top (3) saboteurs, create an action plan for limiting its hold on you. In addition, give each saboteur a name and draw a picture of it.

1st Saboteur Name _____

Draw a picture of it:

Plan for limiting its voice:

_____

_____

_____

_____

_____

_____

2nd Saboteur Name _____

Draw a picture of it:

Plan for limiting its voice:

_____

_____

_____

_____

_____

_____

_____

3rd Saboteur Name _____

Draw a picture of it:

Plan for limiting its voice:

_____

_____

_____

_____

_____

_____

_____

Lesson Two Reflections and Actions to Take

Lesson Three: Get a Reality Check

In the third lesson, we get a reality check via Secret #26.

We are constantly interpreting the things that happen to us through the filter of our beliefs – think of our beliefs as a pair of glasses that have been forming unique lenses since birth. This is great if your beliefs are supportive and they help you take your achievement to the next level; however, not so great if your beliefs are limiting you.

To help ourselves get a reality check, we will use Argyris' *Ladder of Inference*. Remember that awesome former Harvard professor that did a lot of research on how our brain works we discussed in the first lesson? Another one of his tools, the *Ladder of Inference* provides us with a step-by-step process for how a belief is formed. First we'll examine the different rungs on the ladder, then we'll go through the process and observe a belief being formed.

1. The first rung on the ladder is "an event occurs" – the objective record of what happened (something a video camera would capture).

2. Then, we select data from the event – points of interest for each of us.

3. Next, we add meaning to those data points based on our current beliefs and past experiences.

4. We then make assumptions from that meaning.

5. A conclusion is formed.

6. Finally, a belief is solidified.

7. We take action based on the newly formed belief.

Let's use John's recent experience in a meeting as an example of how we can move through the ladder and pretty quickly!

1. For the first step up the ladder – an event occurs. John has an hour-long meeting with his boss and a co-worker in which they discuss updates on his project.

2. After John gives an update on his biggest project, his boss frowns and asks him a question. The data points John pulled were the frown and the question.

3. John then adds meaning to his boss' frown and questions based on his past experiences and already established beliefs – they indicate displeasure to him.

4. Next, John makes an assumption that based on her displeasure, she is disappointed with his project update.

5. Moving up the ladder, John then forms a conclusion that his boss doesn't think he's doing his job well.

6. John then develops the belief that he's not doing his job well and his boss doesn't like him.

7. So he takes action – he avoids his boss. Other behaviors that occur at this stage include gathering evidence to support the newly found belief. If his boss frowns, it's because she's displeased with him; if she gives him another project or reassigns one of his to someone else; it's because she doesn't think he can do his job.

Finally, John heard from several others about how his boss was complimenting him on what a hard worker he was in some of their meetings and he went to speak with her. He asked her for feedback on his work and she told him that he was one of her most valuable employees.

Yikes! John realized that he had created a limiting belief based on his past experiences and how much that had affected him and his stress levels over the last few weeks.

Deepen the Learning

Now that we've learned how we create these beliefs and how much they can affect our entire reality, it's time to deepen the learning – in the following exercises you will deconstruct a belief you've created that's limiting you. You'll have the opportunity to reflect on the current limiting belief and how it is holding you back.

First, you'll work your way through the ladder to deconstruct how that belief was formed. Some individuals find it easier to start at the bottom of the ladder, while others are better able to start at the top and work their way down. Whatever works for you is fine.

After you've deconstructed the belief, you will examine the event that occurred with a different interpretation - one that is potentially more empowering. Much like John did when he realized his belief was greatly limiting him.

Once you've identified what empowering belief you are going to replace your limiting one with – create an action plan for sustaining this new belief.

Secret #26: Get a Reality Check

For this exercise, you will deconstruct a belief you have created. Reflect on a current belief that you have in your life that is holding you back. For example, "My boss doesn't like me," or "My high energy drives others crazy." Once you have that in the forefront of your mind, take it through the following process:

Ladder Rung #1: Event Occurs

Reflect back on the initial event or similar series of events that led to this belief. Describe the event as if you were an unbiased observer.

_____

_____

_____

_____

_____

_____

Ladder Rung #2: Select "Data"

What data did you select from that event to form the basis of your belief?

_____

_____

_____

_____

_____

Ladder Rung #3: Add Meaning

What meaning did you add to that data to form the basis of your belief?

_____

_____

_____

_____

_____

Ladder Rung #4: Assumptions

What assumptions did you make based on the meaning you added to form the basis of your belief?

_____

_____

_____

_____

_____

Ladder Rung #5: Conclusion

What conclusion did you form based on the assumptions you made?

_____

_____

_____

_____

_____

Ladder Rung #6: Belief

What belief did you form based on the conclusion you made?

_____

_____

_____

_____

_____

Ladder Rung #7: Action

What action(s) did you take based on the belief you formed?

_____

_____

_____

_____

_____

Change Perspectives

Look back at the event(s) and mentally go through the rungs of the ladder again, with a different interpretation, one that is more empowering. What did you come up with?

_____

_____

_____

_____

_____

_____

Lesson Three Reflections and Actions to Take

Lesson Four: Choose Your Stories Carefully

You've made it to the final lesson! So far in this section, we've looked at why is it important to think about our thinking; the origin of those negative voices in our head; how our beliefs are formed; and now we'll bring it all together by examining how we can choose the stories that literally define our reality.

This lesson features *Secret #40: Choose Your Stories Carefully*, which is based on the "Narrative Identity Theory" discovered by some really smart researchers. This theory postulates that we integrate our life experiences into an internalized evolving story of the self, which essentially serves as the basis of the formation of our identity.

What does this mean in non-research speak? Your stories create your reality – how you see yourself showing up to the world. Which means that you have the power to create your own reality – freeing isn't it? Although it's also a little scary. If you don't like the story you've created about yourself - you can change it by changing your perspective. It's simple concept but definitely not an easy one to implement.

Deepen the Learning

Let's look at how you can change your story by deepening the learning. In the following exercises, you will choose a limiting story that you currently have. It could be about yourself or about circumstances in your life - something that is holding you back.

The first step is identifying the story. For example, remember Jenny in lesson one? She felt stuck in her office, unable to get a promotion. The story she created was that she had to find a promotion within her current office.

The second step is to identify what benefits the story is bringing you. With Jenny, by saying she was stuck in her office, she was pushing the responsibility away from her - it's not her fault.

The third step is to replace the limiting story with a more empowering one. Jenny decided to view her situation in a different manner – she was choosing to stay there and would widen her perspective to look for positions in other divisions or even outside the company.

Finally, you create a story sustainment plan. Think of ways you can help this new story stick. This step will be unique to you. Jenny decided that she is going to create a goal plan with due dates scheduled into her calendar so as she's checking them off, she will continue to feel motivated in finding a new position.

Now it's your turn – go through all four steps, create an action plan, and get to it.

Secret #40: Choose Your Stories Carefully

For this exercise, you will work on replacing a limiting story with one that is more powerful for you to achieve your goals.

Step 1: Identify the Story

Pick a story you currently have that is keeping you from achieving a specific goal, such as, "I'm stuck in this environment, I can't switch career fields!"

_____

_____

_____

_____

_____

Step 2: Identify the Benefits of this Story

What benefits are this story currently bringing you?

_____

_____

_____

_____

_____

_____

Step 3: Replace the Story with a More Empowering One

What new empowering story can you adopt?

_____

_____

_____

_____

_____

_____

_____

Step 4: Create a "Story Sustainment" Plan

What are some ways you can help this new story "stick"? How do you plan on adopting the new story to remove the obstacles you've created and keep motivated to move forward in achieving your goal(s)?

_____

_____

_____

_____

_____

_____

_____

_____

_____

Lesson Four Reflections and Actions to Take

_____

_____

_____

_____

_____

_____

_____

_____

_____

_____

_____

_____

_____

_____

_____

_____

Conclusion

You've made through the first section! Although all the focus areas are important, this one is absolutely essential to superachieving (and life!)

In this section, we covered metacognition and why it is important to think about your thinking.

Then, we entered the world of the saboteur – those little voices that we hear that are no longer serving us.

In the third lesson, we examined how our beliefs are formed through the *Ladder of Inference* and took a limiting belief, breaking it down, and re-formulating it to be more empowering.

Finally, we realized how we can choose the stories that define our reality and completed a process of changing those stories that have been hindering us in our achievement efforts.

Michael Singer stated, "The day you decide that you are more interested in being aware of your thoughts than you are in the thoughts themselves is the day you will find your way out." Mastering your thoughts is foundational to superachieving (and having a fulfilling life in general.)

In the next section, we look at resilience - which is the capacity to recover quickly from difficulties. As one who wants to change the world, the superachiever often faces frustration and adversity. Resilience is what helps you ride the waves with less frustration and more motivation.

Section Two: Resilience

Welcome to the second section: Resilience! To be a superachiever you need to be resilient.

Resilience is the capacity to recover quickly from difficulties. It's how you view the hardships in your life - do you see them as something that makes you stronger or are they things that just happen to you and you somehow need to survive them?

We don't want to only survive; we also desire to thrive in life. Since superachievers are all about thriving, resilience is a very important aspect of this - which is why it is one of the five main focus areas.

In the first lesson, we cover *Secret #2: Adversity is a Gift*. In this lesson, you will examine how you view adversity and how you can change your viewpoint on adversity to be more successful.

In the second lesson, we cover *Secret #76: Emotions are Data*. Here, we look at emotional intelligence and encourage you to change your perspective on emotions, viewing them as data and providing you with strategies for analyzing the information in that data.

In the final lesson, we cover *Secret #14: Seek Internal Fulfillment*. In this lesson, you will explore the "I'll Be Happy When" syndrome and create a plan for being happy now.

Lesson One: Adversity is a Gift

Welcome to the first lesson on resilience where we closely examine *Secret #2: Adversity is a Gift.*

Superachievers have a healthy viewpoint on adversity enabling them to supercharge their achievement efforts. Making it through a tough situation helps an individual grow in self-confidence. In addition, oftentimes what we initially see as an adverse situation ends up being a blessing in disguise – perhaps pointing us on a different path in life, one that we were meant to take.

Walt Disney stated, "All the adversity I've have had in my life, all my troubles and obstacles, have strengthened me. You may not realize it when it happens but a kick in the teeth may be the best thing in the world for you."

Superachievers see adversity as a gift and a learning opportunity. We may not always have this perspective in the midst of adversity; however, in the end, we look at the hardships that have occurred in our lives and rather than allowing them to break us, we use them growth opportunities.

Deepen the Learning

For the exercises this lesson, you will first identify three times in your life that you have faced adversity. Then for each time you identified, you will ask yourself: 1. What happened?; 2: How am I a better person or how am I in a better place in life because of this adversity that I experienced? What was the gift?

Finally, you will create a plan to make it a habit to ask yourself these questions as you are going through adversity. Sometimes your answer will be – I can't see the gift right now, but I know there is one and it will reveal itself when I'm ready.

Secret #2: Adversity is a Gift

For this exercise, identify three times in your life that you have faced adversity. For each time of adversity, answer the following questions:

Time of Adversity #1

What happened?

_____

_____

_____

_____

_____

_____

_____

Describe how you are a better person or are in a better place in life because of the adversity you faced. What was the gift it gave you?

_____

_____

_____

_____

_____

_____

_____

Time of Adversity #2

What happened?

_____

_____

_____

_____

_____

_____

_____

Describe how you are a better person or are in a better place in life because of the adversity you faced. What was the gift it gave you?

_____

_____

_____

_____

_____

_____

_____

Time of Adversity #3

What happened?

_____

_____

_____

_____

_____

_____

_____

_____

Describe how you are a better person or are in a better place in life because of the adversity you faced. What was the gift it gave you?

_____

_____

_____

_____

_____

_____

_____

Lesson One Reflections and Actions to Take

Lesson Two: Emotions Are Data

Welcome to the second lesson on resilience! In this lesson, we explore our emotions.

Superachievers are emotionally intelligent - we emote when we need to and, in turn, we do not allow our emotions to control us. We understand that our emotions are simply messages - bringing attention to what we need to know. Our thoughts, consciously or unconsciously, create our emotions.

Emotions are triggered based on that sub-programming that we examined in the second lesson in the section on mindset – Don't listen to the negative voices!

Let's look at how this occurs. First, information is received through the five senses. The brain then does a quick search to pull up a previous response and then goes with it. It all about energy conservation for the brain folks!

By seeing our emotions as data, we're able to become an observer of our reactions. This gives us an opportunity to examine them to determine what the appropriate response should be rather than simply reacting.

Deepen the Learning

To retrain your automatic reaction, it takes practice – so let's deepen the learning.

For lesson two you will identify three strong emotions that you have felt in the past 30 days. For each of the emotions go through the following process: What happened?; How did your thoughts create that emotion?; and How can you use this to inform your response the next time you feel this emotion? Finally, you will identify a strategy for stopping yourself in the moment – to move into observer mode – and respond accordingly. Then, practice, practice, practice!

Secret #76: Emotions Are Data

For this exercise, identify three strong emotions that you have felt in the past 30 days. For each emotion, answer the following questions:

Emotion #1_____

What happened?

_____

_____

_____

_____

_____

_____

How did your thoughts create that emotion?

_____

_____

_____

_____

_____

_____

How can you use this to inform your response the next time this you feel this emotion?

_____

_____

_____

_____

_____

_____

Emotion #2_____

What happened?

_____

_____

_____

_____

_____

_____

How did your thoughts create that emotion?

_____

_____

_____

_____

_____

_____

How can you use this to inform your response the next time this you feel this emotion?

_____

_____

_____

_____

_____

_____

Emotion #3_____

What happened?

_____

_____

_____

_____

_____

_____

How did your thoughts create that emotion?

_____

_____

_____

_____

_____

_____

How can you use this to inform your response the next time this you feel this emotion?

_____

_____

_____

_____

_____

_____

Lesson Two Reflections and Actions to Take

Lesson Three: Seek Internal Fulfillment

Welcome to the third lesson for resilience, where we discuss the "I'll Be Happy When" (IBHW) syndrome. This is a big one for superachievers because it's easy to get addicted to achieving, allowing it to become a part of your identity.

It becomes a real problem when you continue going bigger and bigger to get the next accolade. Before you know it, you're accomplishing goals you had no intention of pursuing in the first place.

If you find yourself saying you'll be happy when you get that promotion or that degree or anything else, then it's time to stop reflect on what's going on. We all suffer from the IBHW syndrome from time to time - the important thing is not to live in it.

As superachievers, we seek internal fulfillment. This is the satisfaction or happiness in fully developing one's ability or character. When you are internally fulfilled, you enjoy the journey - not just the destination. It's time to be happy with who you are now and what you've already accomplished. This is an attitude of gratitude.

Deepen the Learning

Let's deepen the learning for this lesson by looking at your problems versus your blessings.

This lesson's exercises ask you to identify areas of your life in which you are telling yourself "I'll be happy when" then re-train your thoughts to focus on being happy now. This is a process – more of a journey rather than a destination.

- The first step in the process involves recalling three problems in the last 30 days that you have faced and felt frustrated or unhappy about.

- The second step is to identify three blessings during the same time for which you feel grateful.

- Finally, look at the difference in your perspective between the two scenarios and how can you bring this perspective into your life to be happy now. Add to your action plan how you plan on sustaining this new perspective.

Secret #14: Seek Internal Fulfillment

What are some areas of your life in which you are telling yourself "I'll be happy when…"?

_____

_____

_____

_____

_____

Let's work on re-training your thoughts to focus on being happy now. Think back to the last (30) days. Recall (3) problems you faced that frustrated you and made you feel unhappy.

_____

_____

_____

_____

_____

_____

Now, recall (3) events that made you feel grateful.

_____

_____

_____

_____

_____

_____

What is the difference in your perspective between the two different scenarios? How can you bring this perspective into your life to be happy now?

_____

_____

_____

_____

_____

_____

_____

Lesson Three Reflections and Actions to Take

Conclusion

Congratulations! You've completed the second section on resilience.

Carl Jung summed up resilience perfectly in his quote, "I am not what happened to me, I am what I choose to become." Wow – that's powerful!

In the first lesson, we covered *Secret #2: Adversity is a Gift.* In this lesson, you had the opportunity to explore the perspective that adversity truly is a gift and a learning opportunity.

In the second lesson, we covered *Secret #76: Emotions are Data.* Here, we examined emotional intelligence and how our emotions are messages in relation to those programs we've developed in our subconscious.

In the final lesson, we covered *Secret #14: Seek Internal Fulfillment.* In this lesson, you explored ways in which you can choose to be happy now.

Now on to the next section where we examine the importance of connection in the life of the superachiever – not only to help you achieve your goals, but also to support you emotionally in your personal and professional development journey.

Section Three: Connection

Congratulations, you've made it to the third section on connection! So far you've worked hard on changing your mindset and increasing your resilience. Now we'll look at the importance of connection.

In the first lesson, we cover *Secret #55: Connection with Others is Nonnegotiable*. In this lesson, you will have the opportunity to examine your connections with others via your network and identify changes you are going to make in order to progress your achievement efforts.

In the second lesson, we cover two secrets, *Secret #23: Get a Fan Club*; and *Secret #70: Call an Intervention*. Here, you will scrutinize your current support system and the designed interventions you have with them. Then you will create an action plan for improving both areas.

In the third lesson, we cover *Secret #27: Find a Champion*. For this one, you will identify one or more champions that can help you get to where you want to go much faster than if you were on your own.

In the final lesson, we cover several secrets: *Secret #41: Be Selective of the Company You Keep*; *Secret #56: Beware of Energy Vampires;* and *Secret #72: Watch Out for Cling-ons!* Here, you will learn just how important it is to be selective in the company that you keep while conducting an analysis of those individuals you allow in your life.

Lesson One: Connecting With Others Is Non-Negotiable

Welcome to the first lesson on connection! Superachieving can be very lonely if we don't allow ourselves to connect with others.

Our connections are what make us better human beings and allow us to accomplish much more. As humans, we need others – we're social animals. This is even more true for superachievers - others can help us achieve our goals more quickly in a myriad of ways.

Deepen the Learning

Let's deepen the learning on connection. In the exercises for this lesson, you will conduct a network analysis on yourself, identifying the individuals in your network. Then, you will do a gap analysis for any gaps in your network and create an improvement plan.

Secret #55: Connection with Others is Nonnegotiable

Conduct a "network analysis" on yourself by identifying individuals in your network. Examine your network by asking yourself these questions:

Is your network big, small, or somewhere in-between?

_____

_____

_____

If your network is big, how are you able to maintain it?

_____

_____

_____

Regardless of the size of your network, are there individuals in it that will help you reach your goals? How so? (Are they in the industry you want? Have the position you want?, and so on.)

_____

_____

_____

_____

_____

_____

Regardless of the size of your network, are you able to have deep vs. surface level relationships with a good portion of your network?

_____

_____

_____

_____

What have you offered those in your network? (Because it is important we give back to others.)

_____

_____

_____

_____

_____

_____

What have individuals in your network helped you with? (Because it is important that you also are able to receive from others.)

_____

_____

_____

_____

_____

_____

Are there any gaps in your network? For example, do you need to add some individuals to help you reach a particular goal? Are there some individuals that have taken more than they've given you? Do you need to further develop some of your relationships?

Create an improvement plan for further building your network:

_____

_____

_____

_____

_____

_____

_____

_____

_____

_____

_____

Lesson One Reflections and Actions to Take

Lesson Two: Get A Fan Club

Welcome to lesson two where we examine your current support system for your superachievement efforts.

Some superachievers try to go it alone thinking others hold them back. Having a support system, also known as a fan club, as well as designed interventions with them, will help you take on the world and lift you up when you are facing the inevitable disappointments along your journey. Obviously, this is a not a one-way street – you do the same for others.

What is a fan club? It can be a team of loved ones made up of people you've chosen to include in your life that bring you joy and love and help you surge forward toward your dreams.

A good fan club member will never hold you back in a negative manner – if someone in your life is constantly criticizing you or belittling you it's time to limit your exposure to them. We'll get to that in lesson four.

It is also important that we have designed interventions with our supporting fan club. Calling an intervention means bringing in help from others to get you back on course. Ultimately it means asking for help AND receiving it which is something your average person is not willing to do.

Superachievers know that there are times when we need help getting past an obstacle (most often ourselves) to maximize our achieving potential.

What does this look like? We'll use James as an example. James knows that when he holes up in his office and he's focused on creating stuff that sometimes he needs to be reminded to take a break. He has set up an intervention with his fan club members that if they see him working away in his office for hours, forgetting to eat and even go to the bathroom, that they have permission to make him take a break.

Deepen the Learning

There are a number of exercise this lesson to help you deepen the learning. First, you'll examine your support system and create an action plan for how you are going to change the membership of your fan club. Then go through a similar process for your interventions.

Take some time to reflect and go through these questions. Then set an action plan and do it!

Secret #23: Get a Fan Club

Look at your superachiever supporters. Who's in your fan club and how do they support you?

_____

_____

_____

_____

_____

_____

_____

_____

Which individual(s) in your fan club is super at helping you be a better person? How do they help you?

_____

_____

_____

_____

_____

_____

_____

Which individual(s) in your fan club really isn't a fan? Who do you need to move to the outer circle of your network or perhaps remove all together?

_____

_____

_____

_____

_____

If your fan club isn't what you'd like it to be, how are you going to change it?

_____

_____

_____

_____

_____

Secret #70: Call an Intervention

What types of interventions have you had to call in the past?

_____

_____

_____

_____

_____

What prearranged interventions do you have with others? If you don't have any, what will you set up? Who in your fan club will you designate to run the intervention if and when it is needed?

_____

_____

_____

_____

_____

_____

_____

_____

How can you call in an intervention sooner when you feel stuck?

_____

_____

_____

_____

_____

_____

_____

Lesson Two Reflections and Actions to Take

Lesson Three: Find A Champion

Welcome to lesson three where we focus on champions. Champions are those individuals that can help you get where you want to go much faster than you would on your own. They are people who have walked the path before you - those who are where you want to be.

Champions can serve as mentors; however, their true purpose is to help pull you up to where they are or at least closer to them than you would be if you were going it alone. A champion's role is to introduce you to his or her network and to be the recognized name endorsing you.

Jan is a great example of utilizing champions - without exception every major thing she's accomplished in her life she's had a champion or two to help her.

Jan recently identified a promotion she wanted in her organization. She found an executive woman in a role that she eventually wanted to be in and asked her to be her mentor (since asking her to be a champion would have been a bit weird!) The woman agreed and through Jan's work with her and the individual's she met in the woman's network, within twelve months, she had that promotion she had set her sights for.

Deepen the Learning

Let's deepen the learning by reflecting on your past experiences of achieving your goals. First, identify who served as a champion for you. Hint: you may not have realized it at the time! In what way did they champion you?

Next, look at where you want to be as far as achieving your goals and ask yourself – who can champion me in this goal?

Finally, develop an action plan for approaching this champion to help you move forward more quickly in your goals and then do it!

Secret #27: Find a Champion

Reflect on your past experiences of achieving your goals. Who has served as a champion for you? In what way did they champion you?

_____

_____

_____

_____

_____

Who is where you currently want to be as far as achieving your goals? How can they serve as a champion for you?

_____

_____

_____

What is your action plan for approaching this champion to help you move forward more quickly in your goals?

_____

_____

_____

_____

_____

_____

Lesson Three Reflections and Actions to Take

Lesson Four: Be Selective of the Company You Keep

Welcome to our final lesson on connection. This lesson is about examining those individuals in your inner circle. These individuals may or may not also be in your fan club - that can actually be an entirely different group altogether.

As a superachiever, your mindset and your energy are the foundation for your achievement efforts, and as such, they must be vigilantly guarded.

Jim Rohn stated we are the average of the five people we spend most of our time with. Knowing this, superachievers are strategic with whom they spend time. Do you want to be a millionaire? If so, do you have an innovative millionaire or two in your five? They don't have to be close, personal friends – it can be someone you study from afar.

The important thing to remember is whatever goals you've set for yourself, you need to ensure that the individuals you spend your time with (in person or studying them) will have a positive influence on your dreams.

Another concern is energy vampires - those people that seem to suck the life out of us after we we've spent some time with them - they could be family members, friends, or work colleagues. They often leave us feeling tired, cranky, and emotionally empty after sometimes only a few minutes in our presence. Get these people out of your life (or severely limit your exposure to them)!

Finally watch out for "cling-ons" - these are individuals who recognize a good thing when they see it and catch a ride on the coattails of the superachiever while offering nothing in return. Cling-ons are not to be confused with individuals who come to learn from the superachiever such as a mentor/mentee relationship or even a champion type relationship. Cling-ons simply want to benefit from the achievements of the superachiever or be associated with the reputation of a person in the know.

Deepen the Learning

Let's deepen the learning and conduct an analysis on how selective you are with the company you keep.

In the first step, you will examine your five and whether they help or hinder you in your achievement efforts. Then decide on any changes you will make and add it to your action plan.

Next, identify any energy vampires lurking in your midst and develop a plan for either limiting your exposure to them or removing them from your life all together.

Finally, examine your interactions for any cling-ons in your life – people who are taking more from you than you are receiving from them. Decide what changes are you going to make to protect yourself from them as well as being more aware of them in the future.

Secret #41: Be Selective of the Company You Keep

Jim Rohn stated that we are the average of the five people that we spend the most of our time with – who are your five people? Describe them.

_____

_____

_____

_____

_____

_____

_____

Do these individuals help or hinder you from achieving your goals?

_____

_____

_____

_____

_____

If your goal is to become a millionaire, you need to spend a good portion of your time hanging out with millionaires. Using this reasoning, what changes do you need to make to your "5" in order to be more successful?

_____

_____

_____

_____

_____

_____

_____

Secret #56: Beware of Energy Vampires

Is there anyone that you spend your time with and you walk away feeling completely drained? If so, how are you going to limit your exposure to them?

_____

_____

_____

_____

_____

_____

_____

Secret #72: Watch Out for "Cling-ons"

Is there anyone currently in your life that is taking more from you than you are receiving from them? If so, what changes are you going to make to protect yourself from them as well as be more aware of them in the future?

_____

_____

_____

_____

_____

_____

_____

_____

_____

Lesson Four Reflections and Actions to Take

Conclusion

Congratulations, you've completed the third section on connection! You examined your connections with others in several ways and hopefully have decided to make a few changes for the better.

In the first lesson, we covered *Secret #55: Connection with Others is Nonnegotiable*. In this lesson, you examined your network and developed a plan to improve it.

In the second lesson, we covered two secrets, *Secret #23: Get a Fan Club*; and *Secret #70: Call an Intervention*. In this lesson, you looked at your current support system and the designed interventions you have with them and created an action plan for improving both areas.

In the third lesson, we covered *Secret #27: Find a Champion*. For this one, you identified one or more champions that can help you get to where you want to go and came up with ideas for approaching them.

In the final lesson, we covered several secrets - *Secret #41: Be Selective of the Company You Keep*; *Secret #56: Beware of Energy Vampires;* and *Secret #72: Watch Out for Cling-ons!* Here, you learned just how important it is to be selective in the company you keep and decided on some changes you will make in this area.

Our connections are what make us better human beings and superachievers. In the next section, our focus turns to how we are preparing our mind, body, and souls for the accomplishment of our goals – self-care.

Section Four: Self-Care

Welcome to the fourth section on Self-Care! To achieve your goals, it is important to take care of yourself first – mind, body, and soul.

If you've ever traveled on airplane, the flight crew requests that you put the oxygen mask on yourself first before helping others. This translates well into life because if you don't take care of yourself first, then you're not able to help others.

In the first lesson, we cover *Secret #30: Nurture Mind, Body, and Soul.* In this lesson, you will examine how you currently tend to your own needs and set a plan for improving your self-nurturing.

In the second lesson, we cover two secrets, *Secret #52: My Body is My Temple; and Secret #76: Listen to Your Body.* Here, we gain gratitude for this vehicle of life and create both check-in and intervention strategies for ensuring we keep our body running smoothly in support of our achievement efforts.

Surprisingly, in the final lesson, we cover *Secret #54: Don't Have Enough Time? Bulls%#@!* Curious on why a lesson on time management is included in the Self-Care section? Well, in this lesson, you will explore how you can manage your time better to ensure that self-care is a priority.

Lesson One: Nurture Mind, Body, and Soul

For our first lesson in this section, we focus on the importance of nurturing your mind, body, and soul. To be a superachiever in all your awesomeness you need to be intentional in how you nurture your mind, body, and soul.

Nurturing your mind means not only continually learning, but also how you grow your wisdom. Are you gaining wisdom from the experiences you have, thus making you a better human being?

Nurturing your body seems obvious; however, what is the first thing we tend to let go when we get busy? We may skip exercising or go through the fast food drive to grab something easy.

Nurturing your soul means that, regardless of your religious or spiritual beliefs or lack thereof, there's a human side to each of us that needs to be tended to. To be loved - to love, to be appreciated, and to enjoy the beauty of life around us.

Deepen the Learning

For this lesson, we will deepen the learning by examining how you currently nurture yourself: mind, body, and soul. First, you will explore what you are currently doing to nurture your mind - make sure and focus on gaining wisdom in addition to knowledge.

Next, what are you currently doing to nurture your body? How are you making your health a priority? Finally, what are you doing to nurture your spirit? Do you go for walks in nature? Look at beautiful scenery? Listen to moving music?

Once you decide what you are currently doing in each area, you will identify how you can step up your game, develop an action plan, and then do it.

Secret #30: Nurture Mind, Body, and Soul

What are you currently doing to nurture your mind (focusing on gaining wisdom, in addition to knowledge)?

_____

_____

_____

_____

What can you do to step up your game in nurturing your mind?

_____

_____

_____

_____

What are you currently doing to nurture your body?

_____

_____

_____

_____

What can you do to step up your game in nurturing your body?

_____

_____

_____

_____

_____

What are you currently doing to nurture your soul?

_____

_____

_____

_____

What can you do to step up your game in nurturing your soul?

_____

_____

_____

_____

Lesson One Reflections and Actions to Take

Lesson Two: My Body Is My Temple

Welcome to the second lesson of this section! Your body is so important to superachieving that it gets his own full lesson. We often don't realize just how important our body is to superachieving until we reach a point of exhaustion or illness and we are forced to slow down.

Here's the problem. We know how to take care of ourselves - information on health is abundantly available. Yet we don't often put this incredible knowledge to use.

We cannot take our bodies for granted - if your body is not healthy you can't achieve your highest potential - it's that simple. The body is an amazing instrument as it can communicate with you in several ways on its status. Tired? You need rest. Hungry? You need nourishment. Sluggish? You need to get moving.

Superachievers are very aware of the body's amazing ability to communicate what is going on and we check in regularly to determine if we need to change our current course of action - unless of course we are due for an intervention from our fan club as we discussed in the third section.

How do we check in with our bodies? This is an individual process. We each need to come up with a process that works for us.

Deepen the Learning

There are several exercises to deepen the learning this lesson. The first exercise is gratitude for your body – you will take some time to appreciate everything your body does for you by writing out a list of statements of gratitude in honor of your body. If you're groaning at this point - there is a strategy behind this, so please do your best.

Once you have more clarity on all that your body does for you, you will focus on how can you take better care of it. How can you check in with it? If you don't currently check in with your body, how do you plan to start?

Finally, what interventions have you created or will you create to ensure you maintain this very important habit? Create an action plan and do it!

Secret #52: My Body is My Temple

Take some time to appreciate everything your body does for you. Write out a list of 50 statements of gratitude in honor of your body.

1.	26.
2.	27.
3.	28.
4.	29.
5.	30.
6.	31.
7.	32.
8.	33.
9.	34.
10.	35.
11.	36.
12.	37.
13.	38.
14.	39.
15.	40.
16.	41.
17.	42.
18.	43.
19.	44.
20.	45.
21.	46.
22.	47.
23.	48.
24.	49.
25.	50.

Now that you have more clarity on all your body does for you, how can you take better care of it?

_____

_____

_____

_____

_____

Secret #75: Listen to Your Body

How do you check in with your body? If you don't currently check in with your body, how do you plan to start?

_____

_____

_____

_____

_____

What interventions have you created (or will you create) to ensure you maintain this important habit?

_____

_____

_____

_____

_____

Lesson Two Reflections and Actions to Take

Lesson Three: Don't Have Enough Time? Bulls%#@!

Welcome to the next lesson where we explore time management.

What on earth does time management have to do with self-care? If you don't properly manage your time and focus on your priorities, your self-care suffers. Saying "I'm too busy" has become a badge of importance or martyrdom for people in our society. They like to claim that there just isn't enough time in the day to accomplish all their responsibilities.

Not true! We make time for what is important. We also spend too much time on stuff that isn't important and really doesn't need to be on our to do list. How much time are you wasting on stuff that doesn't align with your priorities in life?

Unfortunately, when we get busy, the first thing we usually drop is our self-care. If you find yourself saying that you don't have time to exercise or you don't have time to prep a healthy lunch before work what you're saying to yourself is that your health is not a priority.

Deepen the Learning

Let's deepen the learning and examine what stories you tell yourself about your schedule and your self-care. In these exercises, you will determine how to better make self-care a priority and how you can manage your time for effectively to do so. You will then set an action plan and add it to your schedule.

Secret #54: Don't Have Enough Time? Bulls%#@!

What stories do you tell yourself about your schedule and your self-care? Is self-care a priority for you?

_____

_____

_____

_____

_____

How can you better manage your time to include more self-care?

_____

_____

_____

_____

_____

_____

_____

What specific changes will you implement over the next 30 days?

_____

_____

_____

_____

_____

_____

_____

Lesson Three Reflections and Actions to Take

Conclusion

Congratulations, you've completed Section Four: Self-Care - where you reinforced the idea that you need to take care of yourself first to superachieve.

In the first lesson, we covered *Secret #30: Nurture Mind, Body, and Soul.* In this lesson, you examined how well you currently tend to your own needs and set a plan for improving your self-nurturing.

In the second lesson, we covered two secrets, *Secret #52: My Body is My Temple; and Secret #76: Listen to Your Body.* Here, we gained gratitude for this vehicle of life and created both check-in and intervention strategies for ensuring we make our body our highest priority.

In the final lesson, we covered *Secret #54: Don't Have Enough Time? Bulls%#@!* In this lesson, you had the opportunity to explore how you can manage your time better to ensure that self-care is a priority.

You are about to enter the final section – Self-Development! Let's do this!

Section Five: Self-Development

Welcome to our final section on Self-Development! The common thread between all superachievers interviewed for the Quit Bleeping Around® Podcast is that they are always learning. Always.

Self-development is the path that takes a superachiever from good to great to exceptional and it is a life long journey.

In the first lesson, we cover *Secret #57: For Goodness' Sake, Get Some Coaching!* In this lesson, you will examine where you are in your self-development journey and create an action plan for moving forward.

In the second lesson, we cover *Secret #25: Enlighten Me!* Here, you are introduced to the "Enlighten Me" game, a strategy for taking the learning from every moment in life (while reducing your frustration in the process).

In the final lesson, we cover *Secret #31: Study Your Greats*. In this lesson, you will look at how you've learned from your current greats and identify others to take you to the next level.

Lesson One: For Goodness' Sake, Get Some Coaching!

Welcome to the first lesson on Self-Development, where you will have the opportunity to examine where you are in your personal and professional development journey.

Superachievers are all about self-development. They ask themselves - how can I make myself even better? Okay now that I'm better how can I make myself great? Now that I'm great how can I be even more exceptional?

To superachieve we need to constantly develop ourselves and not just our technical skills. One's ability to relate with others is essential to achieving anything in life, so "soft skills" are more important than the technical ones.

Deepen the Learning

To deepen the learning this lesson, you will gauge the status of your self-development journey, determine what you want to improve upon in the next 30 days, and develop an action plan. It is important to be specific here, such as I will complete the next four lessons in *Five Areas of Focus* by [enter date here]. Make your goals S.M.A.R.T.!

Part of that action plan is deciding what you are going to do each day for 15 days. At the end of those 15 days, you will assess your progress and create a plan for the remaining 15 days.

While it's important to have big picture goals of your development, it is also important that you continue to follow this 30-day plan process with the 15-day reassessment within each plan to ensure that you remain on top of your development efforts.

Feel free to adjust the number of days in your plan as long as too much time doesn't pass before each reassessment and plan adjustment. Now, get to it!

Secret #57: For Goodness' Sake, Get Some Coaching!

Do you currently have an Individual Development Plan (IDP)? For life, not just work? If so, what is it? If not, why not?

_____

_____

_____

_____

How do you want to develop yourself over the next 30 days? What do you want to learn (make sure you include both technical and "soft" skills).

_____

_____

_____

_____

_____

_____

_____

_____

_____

Identify specifically what you will work on each day for the next 15 days to ensure you develop in the identified areas. At the end of the 15 days, assess where you are and then create a plan for the next 15 days.

Day 1:

Day 2:

Day 3:

Day 4:

Day 5:

Day 6:

Day 7:

Day 8:

Day 9:

Day 10:

Day 11:

Day 12:

Day 13:

Day 14:

Day 15:

Take time assess where you are and then set the plan for the next 15 days.

Day 16:

Day 17:

Day 18:

Day 19:

Day 20:

Day 21:

Day 22:

Day 23:

Day 24:

Day 25:

Day 26:

Day 27:

Day 28:

Day 29:

Day 30:

While it is important to have "big picture" goals of your development for the year, it is also important that you continue to follow this 15-day plan, assess, 15-day plan, and so on, to ensure that you remain on top of your development efforts. Feel free to adjust the number of days; however, make sure that too much time doesn't pass before each reassessment.

Lesson One Reflections and Actions to Take

_____

_____

_____

_____

_____

_____

_____

_____

_____

_____

_____

_____

_____

_____

_____

_____

_____

_____

Lesson Two: Enlighten Me!

In the second lesson, we explore the Enlighten Me! method for self-development. Superachievers know that we can learn 24/7 – in each waking hour, we can work on expanding our mindset and learning about the world around us.

In this lesson, we introduce you to *Secret #25: Enlighten Me!* This is a very simple yet profound technique to further develop yourself that involves pretending that everyone else around you is enlightened, you're not, and you want to learn how to be enlightened.

What does this look like? For every situation in which you find yourself, you ask "what is this person teaching me right now" or "what is this situation teaching me right now?"

We'll use Larry as an example of how this works. He has recently begun practicing the Enlighten Me! method. Larry has a colleague at work that he finds himself constantly frustrated with because she finishes his sentences for him – and often in a completely different direction than he intended to go.

He found himself in another one of these conversations with her the other day. When he felt his frustration levels rising, he stopped himself and asked, "What is Dena teaching me right now?" Larry realized that the specific words Dena was using to finish his sentences provided great insight into her perceptions on the topic at hand and he could use this information to reformulate how he presented the issue to her, thus changing the entire outcome of the situation.

Larry went from being frustrated to fascinated with how much he could learn by simply becoming curious.

Deepen the Learning

It's time to deepen the learning and start using the Enlighten Me! method.

First, you will recall the last person, situation, or circumstances that frustrated you, then practice the Enlighten Me! method. Next step is to make practicing Enlighten Me! a habit – to find a way you can remind yourself when you're in the moment that you believe would benefit you to learn from.

Secret #25: Enlighten Me!

Recall the last person, situation, or circumstances that frustrated you. What was the lesson? Dig deep if you initially have trouble!

_____

_____

_____

_____

_____

_____

_____

How can you make practicing Enlighten Me! a habit? In other words, how can you remind yourself to engage in finding the learning in any situation?

_____

_____

_____

_____

_____

_____

_____

_____

_____

_____

Lesson Two Reflections and Actions to Take

Lesson Three: Study Your Greats

What better way to pull yourself up quicker into accomplishing your dreams than to study those whom have gone before you? In the third lesson, we look at studying your greats.

Greats can be people you know or people you've studied from afar. Essentially they are individuals who have accomplished what we hope to achieve. As superachievers, we study them - we read their books, consume their website, watch their interviews, and explore any other media that we have available to us, to examine what they did to become successful.

The benefits of studying your greats are obvious, so we don't need to go into them - the question is how deep do you go in studying them?

Have you ever thought of contacting your greats? What about sending them an email, asking them a question or two, or for 10 minutes of their time? What's the worst that could happen? They say no or don't respond at all? Big deal!

Deepen the Learning

Let's look at how you can deepen the learning for this lesson. First, you will identify current greats and what you are doing to study them. Then, you will go deeper in your study of them to include potentially reaching out and contacting them.

Once you come up with ways you want to expand your development in this area, you will create an action plan and implement it.

Secret #31: Study Your Greats

Who are your current greats and what are you doing to study them?

_____

_____

_____

_____

_____

_____

How you can go deeper in your study of them? Make sure to include your ideas in your updated development plan.

_____

_____

_____

_____

_____

_____

_____

_____

_____

Lesson Three Reflections and Actions to Take

Conclusion

Congratulations! You have completed the final section of this guidebook on self-development. Essentially, this entire course has been for your self-development, so kudos to you!

Brian Tracy stated, "If you wish to achieve worthwhile things in your personal and career life, you must become a worthwhile person in your own self-development." Let's recap your efforts in this section.

In the first lesson, we covered *Secret #57: For Goodness' Sake, Get Some Coaching!* In this lesson, you examined where you are in your self-development journey and created your first 30-day action plan for moving forward.

In the second lesson, we covered *Secret #25: Enlighten Me!* Here, you were introduced to the "Enlighten Me" game, a strategy for taking the learning from every moment in life (especially the frustrating ones!).

In the final lesson, we covered *Secret #31: Study Your Greats*. In this lesson, you looked at how you've learned from your current greats and identified others to take you to the next level.

You have one final portion of the guidebook – the conclusion, aptly titled, "Bringing It All Together."

Bringing It All Together

Congratulations! You have completed the Five Areas of Focus for Superachieving guidebook and have begun the life-long journey of working on the concepts we've covered.

Over the five sections, we've examined the five areas of focus that will help you supercharge your achievement efforts. They are mindset, resilience, connection, self-care, and self-development.

You have had the opportunity to do some deep reflection in each of the focus areas and I hope you took the time to do so. This is transformative life-changing stuff here!

The biggest secret of all is to enjoy the journey. Take the time to enjoy the process of superachieving - what you learn and who you become are so much more important than how many trophies, degrees, promotions, and so on, that you collect.

Finally, I want to leave you with this - it's time to show up fully and embrace who you are. Unleash your superachiever awesomeness to make this world a better place.

Happy superachieving! Do something awesome today!

Christina Eanes

Now...

Quit bleeping around, and get to it!

Made in the USA
Middletown, DE
20 May 2017